Listener

Samuel Amadon

SOLID OBJECTS

NEW YORK

SOLID OBJECTS

P. O. Box 296

New York, NY 10113

For Liz Countryman

My mouth doth water, and my breast doth swell,
My tongue doth itch, my thoughts in labour be:
Listen then, lordings, with good eare to me,
For of my life I must a riddle tell.

—Sidney

And I feel
"I"
is too small for me.
Some other body is bursting out.

—Mayakovsky

TABLE OF CONTENTS

ONE

LISTENER

Let my ears be part of this. Let me be the listener.
I'll set each word on top of each, as one
Might lay reams of paper to form a staircase,

Opening in my attic, among furnace ducts, cases
Of light bulbs, spools of speaker wire strung
Between boxes and crates where, by myself, I'll speak

And wait for an answer, tense and cold up to
My fingertips or in my fingertips alone. I'll talk
Of the pointlessness of poetry, how it comes to serve

Me less as I use it more, as what pierced and punctured,
Now settles, slants and clears as a palm clears
Brush from a window screen. Let me alone.

Let me talk, as I reorder my books, as I see how far along
I've gotten in reordering them before little partitions
Are put in place, somewhere I stopped between

Junipers or spruces, snow on the sidewalk
Or pollen in the air over the highway, moments I grew
Distracted by the sound of me moving around

In the early hours, asking to be lined up myself, put in
Order myself, by myself, despite all the talk
Of my originality, my reckless transformation,

Now, let me, now that I'm paid to be here,
Now that my accounts rise and fall in predictable
Patterns, now I can say I'm no reader.

These books I have I have only for my shelves. I carry
Them back and forth between rooms and offices,
Between cars and elevators to desks where I lay them

Open and let them be. Listener, I hear myself
Say, do you see pine needles on the ground, on my tires?
The air is shagged with them. They pile

Into pages, like the voice of some person who won't stop
Talking, as he starts in on a story I already know,
Oh how it is difficult then for one who wishes to

Stand alone in the cold, where sounds hold such silence
I feel I could touch them, listener,
As they hang there between us like a grudge.

VAGRANCY IN THE SLOPES

Someone has walked across a skyline view, or down
A pond road into garden and gazebo, where

The feeling I have come back for draws a stick
Across the gravel floor. A certain arbor—how

Collapsible I seem from under its mattress of vines.
Like a pile of blue dress shirts, I've spread. One can

Find more room, and more to do. The days weave
Between air and hours where I'm awake, still

With my face on a pillow, more often on the couch,
Eyes up to the flicker on the ceiling, pulled away

From shore, I listen to dialogue, hear myself in each
Scene. I'm done getting used to things. You know

What I mean. You don't learn how to sit through
Every hour, each moment takes its move, regardless

Of you. I walk a floor laid between glass brick walls—
I stand behind the yellow line while parts of an express

Train pass. Here's someone looking for he knows
Not what. Here's the point to which I've got. All

Places I haven't been, I feed into—I enter rectangles,
Fit in and out of rectangles—I tangle through

My cords, pin myself to mapboards, plot my direction
In electric grids. I can hear something I want to say

Hum on the sides of my face, and as I reach to say it,
I spill out in the wind. I have the wind in view.

HOT TALK

I have a family. I'm on
The faculty. I don't

Walk into innuendos,
Even if they hang

Like spider webs
Between asphalt and trees

On nights when
There's not much

Breeze. When I want
Relief on my lips,

I have a few
Questions. Inflections.

I know your name.
Can you spell it out

With me? Lots of little
Animal landings

Sound on your roof.
Accents. Rhythms.

The world consists of
Moods passing

Rain to snow. Flatness.
When I lost control

Of what I was saying,
It was evening. It was

Going to be
Evening. Days went on

Without explanation.
In a green light,

My tongue was large.
I couldn't help but

Hold it in my mouth.
If I said I was

Leaving, it was
The way I wouldn't.

If I mistook my hand
For yours, I held it

There after
It wasn't the same.

MAD AND NOMAD

In a year of throwing voices into the hot wind
Filling the road with blue and red

Sawhorses blocking the street in a year of
Knowing the correct

Word or where places were as I
Imagined them growing dark like levels

I hadn't reached in a game
I was playing too much time lost to one thing

I should revolve around the lost time give it
The attention I give myself in a year of watching

All the branches fallen in my yard
Fall out of the wind across my attempts to

Focus to keep going a little longer
Wrapped up in a blanket on the porch

In a year of women moving into the house
Across the street each with her turn using

The leafblower in a year of not
Knowing anyone by their faces no matter

What they say their voices come out of
Movies in a year of building

A barricade with magazines and newspapers
I added to it whenever I wasn't paying attention

I set myself to doing nothing in a year of
Not finishing my thought I was circled by a moon or

Several I was clay settled into
A chair opposite myself a part of a pair

I felt as if I'd arrived at lunch not knowing
Whether I should be there but still

This water contains a lemon slice
Floating amid so much ice in a year of

Tornado warnings or in a year of
An actual tornado across the city growing as it

Passes above the man-made lakes
Through the fairgrounds crossing back and forth

Over the river before coming up the hill
And holding at the intersection outside my house

Will I come to the porch to meet it
Or huddle behind my walls

Purpling under green skies in a year of what I can I will
In a moment by speaking forward be

Moving in circles not unlike someone rotating
A lazy susan in search of what's outside

The circumference of their desire in a year of
When I was expected to arrive passing

For a moment before me holding me up rushing in
So late you'll have to forgive me if I'm not myself

ANECDOTE IN MY THROAT

into a loft in the air
I rolled letters

pages that fell from
my height my tree

my tower window
glassing over

a townscape where I type
to the right the left

the words
a pile of dictionaries

bringing forward
what might lay too long

in asking if you've crawled
under my house

dug your way below
pipes and wires

toward the gap
punched in the bricks

elbowed out to what
would I hide there

bristle or silence
you see the days

and which way they go
the bucks clattering

we're exposed
our comfort in things

almost over isn't enough
to stop the tufts of

whatever's up as if
to be taken in in

branches of
a neighbor's trees

a bridge tangled in
its cords sways free

and into view
a taste in my mouth

crisp as chips
left out in the mist

I close my eyes
while I get the gist

FABULOUS CORRIDORS

Will I write to myself? I'm asleep in the library, a stack
Of tiny columns opens in my face, lets me read it. I circle

Around like a boy on his bicycle after dinner. If I don't
Have room for what I pass, I keep looking anyway. My mind

Is at peace, as it settles in, like a colored wedge drops into a pie,
If the answer's right. Bluebirds are like me, moving around

With little dodging feet. I evaluate myself. I feel parched
On a winter's day. I ramble as I read. When the snow perishes

From the yard, I say this must be very hard. The wind
Falls upon me with sounds from the trees. Here I am.

A little faster. How I love my old book. I set it on my knee.
Pages fall through my fingers, like phantoms. Maybe

I dissolve. Maybe I drone outward into night
Blues. On the palmy beach, I take all my words. What starts

As bubble, ends as foam. My name escapes me. I am
In Florida. I put my notes down. I take

My glasses off. I fill my hull. I race an island, as the current
Drives me. I say what I think. There will never be

An end. I hold my book. I check my page. Here I am.
Into alabaster, out of phosphor. I'm no place new.

MY DELINQUENCY

Having to be so without having to be so, I take my seat at the bar.
It's my manner. I'm willful. Absent. Crisp. And cold. I know

where to point my eyes when speaking, when listening, when
the check arrives. I'm having lunch today because

I'm pretty civilized. When I ride the train, I curve
when it curves, and I stop when it rests—after I take a sip, I pause

to take a breath. Here is my theme. I'm late for this. I'm late
for that. I'll ask you to move back

from the billiard table while I take my shot. I hold the cue with
my fingers though my fingers flop. This is

the sweet season. These are salad days. I walk
into the diner, into the park, out onto the rocks above the lake
        in love

with my blue t-shirt, my blue jeans, my watch and my cologne.
I'm happy to talk with you, and I'm happy to be alone.

I find my legs cross at the ankles as I sit in a row
as if with others in a hallway stretching over and out of

corners with empty classrooms, water fountains, lights
dimming off their sensors—I'm all "after school"

and up to chat as I lay my hands down flat to the tiles and look
from side to side in a sequence

of nods and smiles. As often as I like, I get away from myself
toward the talk I'm into, conversations after

the thing, breezing on my daily vacations, unoccupied
in extra time. Come back, come back. The watch on my hand

has no strap. I'm adult, I'm outside, and if it's
a fault, I mean, then the fault is mine. This is how I've dared

all afternoon on the stone steps below the tree
filled with blossoms and bees, waiting for someone who looks
    like

me, after he's casually gone absent from the meeting
room, out for a twirl past my stoop—for me

there's something moored to this business
not through—the sun on our skin and everything due.

TWO

TOMORROWMAN

I am a tomorrowman.

Days runs up and down the veins in my feet, calves, thighs,
And cheeks.

I'm never out of time.

I say enough
When I have too much. Look at me, for instance,

Tomorrow—the day of the hurricane—

How I'll lay piled on the bed,

Where I alone may say what's garbage. Pleasure. Pity. Verse.

I'll be in and out of my head, my mouth, where people's faces
Will roam in herds.

I'll seek fit words.

The circuit of the rain

Will be clean,
Will be a terrible fix, will be

Turning the wind.

Will be what I left in the yard.

Will be less present in that I'll be
Writing it down.

What I'll have, I'll bury. Borrow. Build. And loan.

I'll be available, in and out of my mouth
Will pass

Many people.

I'll be speaking to them. I'll be

Sweet,

And I'll be angry.

I'll want credit for what it is to be.

I'll stand on top of the staircase and ask everyone to see me, while
The storm rages.

*

I saw myself.

I was what my nature wrote. I was a copy.

Electric, and full of fever. A transformer blown. Popped.
Banged.

When I met myself

Again,

I preferred myself.

When cold spots rung my fingers, I was thinking of my future.

Tender,
My future.

Out of cash.

A body on
The floor, afraid of the great silence opening outside the door.

When that day comes, if I have nothing to say, I can still

Speak what I feel.

When that day comes,

I'll feel as much as they say one should.

My particles will buzz like a green screen.

I'll have tracers. In fact,

I have them now. In fact,

I've sung the future into me.

I hold a limb in another time, and when
I listen through it,

I hear the calendar hymn.

*

It is tomorrow.
I listen. I hear. I see tomorrow's stars and planets,

Although

There is a silence between us,

I am able to stand it, as I am able to speak while,
By myself,

Tomorrow's air goes thin.

I breathe my breath with my head in my hair.

All is well.

Take care.

Take care.

I walk around the edge of my land, framing sentences in
Phrases fine,

But in the end I am candid.

I am known for my candor. Follow me,

Though you will not hear me, I finish what I mean
To say.

True. It is nonsense.

Tomorrow has stolen it away.

I had
Tomorrow's thought which wouldn't stay.

A rabbit in the yard whenever I stepped outside.

Now gone.
Now

All this beauty back into beauty flows.

It will stoke
The iridescence of the ocean. It will

Toss stars around the surface of the sky.

Speak in tomorrow's lines.
In tomorrow's time.

*

I have my thoughts, even if I have no sense of them.
I speak in voices,

Try to sing. Listen,

Tomorrow's marble's mixed in red and white.

Tomorrow'll dazzle. It won't delight.

I live in a place that's not my own. The clouds hover

Above
My almost home.

All night, phone calls stop and start. I'm known

For having an eye for a heart.

A mimic in the mirror,
Hear me do my

Hometown boy from a hometown place.

When I look at you, I look

Tomorrow right in the face. I'm tomorrow gone. Tomorrow
Stuck.

I may not drive around town in a big black truck, but

Watch me

Blow through this red light. Tell me

I don't do it right.

*

I do it to myself.
In those crucial productive daytime hours, my hold

On the argument
I am building, the way I planned to build it—it

Gets away from me for how I feel about things,

That's what I make here now, while I lay

Twisty and talky

In my room. I pull my feelings out my fingers.

Out
The hairs on my arms. Out

These boxes, these boxes get
Bent, get loose, and the day I'll take care of it is

Always tomorrow, is

Always as rosy as it is weary, is
Always darting ahead on smooth pillows, sweetest

Bed. It's the recovery.

Maybe there's a half-life to these
Things, and I don't flower quite as bright in the doorway

With a blue-button up, but I like to

Get better.

I don't care

How much. It's tomorrow I keep involved with.

I'm a busy fellow. While the deserts widen,
I let my lawn yellow.

*

Have we met yet? I'm here from tomorrow.
I'm here for tomorrow.

I'm a busy fellow.

I keep up with things.
I check your progress,

Reader,
As you turn over your cheddar and bean burrito.

I like you.

I like that you can tell the difference between when

The microwave door is

Open,
And closed, when a bite

Enters your mouth
Still frozen,

And when it's just a touch cold.

You chew it up either way.
I do that too.

There's something
Nice about things being not so great.

I like that we don't relate.

That we've never gotten along.

That I could be talking aloud
Now like

I'm waiting in the train station,

Thinking
How else it could've gone.

How if I was going to travel by car,

It should've
Been with you. We would've

Gone swiftly,

In the manner in which I read aloud
As I type,

The manner in which one may pass

Into a black forest

After rain,

Wetted by blue, to

Find a house in the sun's clearing has changed a little,

A lot.
And to enter it then, distracted, as a man in thought.

*

As a tomorrowman, I have tomorrow
Things—

My tomorrow limbs in my tomorrow clothes,

The tomorrow words I know.
The tomorrow mind I set forth

Is restorative, is
Enhanced. Is faulty.

Is a restless ache beclouding my stormy face

As days roll in their thunderheads.
As I feast, and am fed.

Apples on the table. Apples

In a basket on my porch, left by whom?

Does it matter,

When the hurricane will collect them, will hold
Them, will

Ring them around the neighborhood?

Everyone will get one.

Tomorrow. They are tomorrow's apples,
And they are sweet.

*

I'll tell you what I've done. Tomorrow,
I've been through it.

I can't stand it.
I can't say it again. And yet, tomorrow, I'll say it,

Tomorrow,

Out of instinct, on rotation,

Happy or unhappy or gone back over or back out of what

I said—
I don't know—I

Don't spell it out in my head.

A page of paper shredded by the rain or
Decayed in a steady

Breeze—my constant

Pacing in speech, and here I am never weary of my melody,

In the hallway, speaking

To myself. It was
The sort of tomorrow when the mailman puts

A stack of magazines

Right into my hand.

Here's
my tomorrow porch, where I pace back and forth.

I want to get better at this. From my green chair,

I divide, man and tomorrow.

I rise and smile and hope to be
Pursued.

A blue jay dies in my yard. I go in my shed, return with
My shovel, when all

The blood goes to my head. Oh! The jay in the bush.

It's June!

Tomorrow is in flower. Each day is
Hotter in the afternoon.

*

I wake up. A bird sounds outside. It is, needless to say,
Tomorrow.

Tomorrow has arrived.

It is
A morning like most. I haven't slept enough.

I walk down the blue stairwell

With the lights still off. I don't feel

Burdened by

My routine.
Making coffee.

Checking on the cat.

Is this

How I thought it would be? I don't know if I've kept
Track of what I thought

Enough.

How do you know if you're hopeful for a future
That's already here?

I feel so
Present I could disappear. In a second now,

I'll walk out

The door, off the porch. I'll call tomorrow's name.

A strange same.

A tomorrow ordinary and not, as I walk down to
The concrete,

Between mind and sky,

And this tomorrow meet.

THREE

MY DOMINATION

I aim the frame, as the night
grows ripe,
as flames feather
about my head, where my face
will soon appear.
I'm living on a swivel, meaning
I've controlled myself, prepared
myself, lost myself,
splintered myself, loaded
myself, bathed
myself, regained myself.
In the silver, studded frame of
a nighttime mirror,
I approach myself. My face.
I come striding out
from the trees, striding
out from the planets.
I look like I've learned
something, turning in flames
in the wind, in the loud fire,
as the twilight's cry
repeats in the fallen leaves.
They sweep over the room.
First, a dry scent,
second, piles raise
over my head,
and third, I feel them
filling and passing
and sweeping
through the ceiling, buildings,
city lines and roadways.

I feel afraid.
I feel my face flicker
as a television or as
an image is
blinked at
or as boughs placed
late in a blaze.

RED CARRYING MOON

A bright obvious, the moon rode clear of my mind, or
Was part of a draft I lifted with out on the patio,

Where a pile of bricks scattered into place in a wall, then
Back to almost a pile. It was like losing

A memory from the effort of pulling it up. These moments
Or some filmy version held (successfully) by feeling

Out the driveway where roads warped a hill,
Dark and open. Things floated as my eyes got comfortable,

The way thoughts cross, equivalent to a path by the river,
Which leaps the river with no warning, no bridge

I noticed as I was walking, caught in a conversation of
Parts not quite perceived, as if I was a boy in

A field where branches bent down to my fingers in a box
Of loose wheels, tiny signs, cardboard limbs,

Cords of string—I can't recall whether I looked up as I
Approached, nor how I saw myself as my own

Toy—the mechanism still in motion in a corner, under
Fictitious lamplight, and though it is faceless,

It lifts, as it turns, a pile of feet, hands, and wings.
I come from the twentieth century. I want to make things.

BLUE VIEWS

I looked down my face quiet and calm
I played a game without

Pronouncing it correctly I found everything
Felt like my head

Worsened beside water poured
Out my mouth around my ear

I was the book
And summer night turned past

My shoulder curled mattress
Wrapped in sheets of my shoulder

I sat in my underwear
Looking at the morning wall I was

Being the book I managed a wealth of colors
Leaning out of windows

White siding betrayed none of the cold
I stood in

All yellow lights
Stairwells hotel pillows bright below my stripes

My fingers were sticky I was
The house quiet I covered my fingers with fruit

I had a torso
Wrapped in clear black plastic sheets

I spoke as no book I wrote
Yellow and red letters between I blurred beside

The blur passing it off as reunion
I leaned above the page I was

Moving back in time a speed
Cinema images rapid over rivers and mirrors

I was found between my flesh my flesh wrapped
A blue white towel out over my back

Like an island would've been blue I was a perfection
Of summer night I pointed

I was naked with a finger in my mouth
A peach in the crook of my elbow

I put a pile of money into my camo vest
I was what falling backwards did to

Definition in the flicker
Spread slickness over like clouds in the sea

I straightened a negotiation in skin and fabric light
A stack of books black jeans folded I let

What I wore stretchmark out
For you to see a light in my eye I was a kitchen

Outside a room smoking I let
An open mouth be where it was I was

No reader I let
My eyes slip greenly in the black air

TO THE DRAINS

I have a dream where someone
takes my mask—as it
hardens into form, it's clear
I can't have it back—now

a thousand miles from my face,
out where prairie snow
crosses into each asphalt ditch,
how it hovers just below

where I watch the road,
green signs along the interstate,
where my being a person cludes
progression. I'm out here.

If nothing I say is lost,
is lost in fact, but layered over
like the mind in my head
that finds a way to never let

it go, as I
wander after vacancies
in the fog, the night—I hold
a hand before my eyes

as if I'd see both here, inside,
where time is what
I'm thinking of in increments,
which pass slower than one'd

expect of a thing relentless at
its work. It's not made up.
A man approaches
with his false French accent.

He says "Marcellus" several times,
and then he's there on our
minds. Our shoes untied.
Mud in all the telephone lines.

I'd like to let it go. Things
leave off. I wake afloat on
finding where the fog
lifted, the night settled in

around my feet. Tell me, is that
how it is? Or do these pairs
twist like cobalt rises out
of cornflower, and cornflower

falls back into shade? I can
gather myself up, as if
there's a knock at the door,
and I step out to the street with its

lots, and porches, and swings. But
when no one's there? I slow inside.
I sit back in my time
with this hollow sound in mind.

PERSONAL QUANTITIES

I have a feeling for
slowing things
though the day goes
on without asking
rains wrap inches
over my next move
the sound of
foliage gray
and white I'm ready to
be caught here
I pull together
my outfit
fluid as groundwater
through soil
I don't have
anything to tell
the rain grows
unhurried over me
the leaves bend
down in measure
and still I want
to go slower
I don't want to lose
anything with
two hands out
in a forest
it falls around
me and I
keep moving
into the rain
thicket sounds

rains a forest
is endless I am
circling myself
hands cupped
together turning
the rain over
oh I am relaxed
deliberate in no
rush and still
not slow enough

I HAVE A BODY

I put my book to my head, remain
Thoughtful. My body so
Round, itself rising up
The street like ants in a flood.
I can't turn
Who I am with what I've read
Now—nor what I plan
To read as the week scraps and piles

Around me, over
Me. I hope it figures my fingers
About my waist, as I
Stand wanting to write another poem
In the kitchen, where
I think I must be growing, but it's
Hard for me to see. Now
I'm standing in line

For my own front door.
I have no book.
Watch my flesh, a body's cheeks
Collect, sustain,
And sit atop each other, as
I transfer what was
Out of place: this
Time has been a mess. I can answer

Your questions, but don't
Ask me to go along with my
Thinking. I have to
Watch. Listen
To. Planes pass all the time,
And they're not visible.
I hear them while I wait to see
Whether these are the ants that burn.

It's information passing up and down
A leg. It's worn bad shoes.
As often as not, I have
No room for the afternoon.
Everything matches.
My fingers freeze as each reflection
Passes, and if I know
The plan, I leave before it hatches.

POEM IN JULY

I felt perfected along the rectangle
By its ragged side

Fences trees and mist dropping
Some space for the flowers

I set an image in my head where
Bushes in their out of focus

Made a green dearth about the door
I wanted to do a book on

Pages left in the heat or rain
But my desire seemingly disappeared

Picked up by a car in the middle of
A pack of cigarettes

This trip into the forest
The trees trading with memory to

Frame the various breaks
The pleasures of small laws cut

Behind the mower with my eyes
Running the grass blades

We don't really get any older
I can see what that means

FOUR

SPY POEM

I don't know how I found you—like
      red dots spread across lines, pages

     before I noticed I
read them as if I read them—like when turns

    of plot arise
      in shows I watch

while thinking how I thought them there—
    as in this passage here—now dear—

      come to where this paragraph goes
      to imagine your name

like your signature— I found you—your style
    in these spots—red

      dots move across
the lines with what you are saying—

    and I may have caught an error,
      but what gets fixed with "cinch" too close

     to "clinch" in article
on Israel—as with rain, its coming

    down pattering
      on how it used

to sound too much the exact thing,
        like same—is your fact—is your fact

            back here—it's disappearing, dear—
            I found you still in one

direction, and not yet gone to what we
        hear in the rain,

            still in its same
fact—you are approaching, brother—

            that's the rain becoming patterned
                as exactly mine patterning

            yours—is that the point to find
you may be what I know slips close *closer*—

            there's more to hear—
            or better throw

it in reverse across the lawn
        whose house—that sound—a garbage can

            crushed by the way—you seem to know
            the route but not the turns—

now dear, before we get this picture of
        you again—how

        you hate not to
be perfect is less sometimes with

someone there to see you hate it—
    it must be lovely to be like

    hair—to have precision
so render your value apparent to

    yourself—but can
        you read with red

ants across the page—you write of
    the self thinking of ways in which

        to appear the self able to
        determine the moment

you traded the feeling of being watched
    for noticing

        you were watching—
you write this like a witness to

    an accident, considering
        your account more and more closely

    until the belief that
memory itself is time, itself is

    that kind of light
        everywhere,

no, none here, then another like
    hair you think you finished sweeping—

I said "brother" in the middle
of the paragraph with

two sweaty trash bags—one crawling with ants—
a story you

tell about how
you split with thinking where it caught

you here—years before—a park bench,
willing to engage in chatter,

considerate, pleasant,
but by most accounts this conversation

does not exist,
not for all these

people on the sidewalk, nor those
possibilities of its width

that were left to you sent forward
by believing you went

faster sent to the ground, broke your own tea
bottle—no one

helped as you came
toward where need was confused for

violence—like when the subway doors
shut on a woman with a box,

the man kicked the wall, said
"they're doing it on purpose"—dear, notice:

first a branch moved,
then several,

a bird coming forward onto
the sidewalk where it meets the walls,

the building—uphill—the building
continued to the store,

which was larger than thought, extending past
corners—voices—

the tomatoes—
behind them there is space for what—

Uruguay turning another
you in sheets of mountain aerie—

resting on the edge of
I have no time for anyone who'd need

the person next
to them, before

deciding they'd fit perfectly
behind the phrase, "now close the door"—

you were late, which made the crowds more
difficult, the same as

if you had nothing to do, but listen:
    the farther store,

        the street empty,
again—I turned, you knocked into

        how far off—was it me moving
           the crowd—have you ever

           noticed it's possible
to forget birds for weeks, concerned with your

        own behavior—
           had nothing to

do with everything else—but
        how bright the light, what you made that—

           the tomatoes you ate baked spoon
           inside each, warmer than

voices you expected further into
        what you couldn't

           see—that night you
write of where rain is as white light

        over red dots, revealing they aren't—
           aren't they—simpler as splatter from

           the tomatoes on your
apparitions—come in, that's a coat rack,

speak, that's a light
switch it loose like

things are supposed to come apart—
there's a selection—is that what

he traces in his pocket—no,
only lining—ask him—

what do we call him—brother—*hey brother
is the lining*

good here—listen,
cinch means clinch, a sound that's dear to—

I don't know how I found you—like
there was a fix in on the fix—

no, that was not hinted,
that door at your touch was enough thesis—

remember you
don't remember

how to play—that's preparation—
like thawing a whole in pieces—

like breathing so you can feel the
elevation—like change

long dead from lack of change or oxygen—
are you thirsty

now, dear—I've had
you unjustly, you feel the time

    like time breaking, acting as if
        asking for just three square instants

    is to ask everything—
you haven't even thought that far in far

    too long—brother,
        it's not who asks

the questions, but that you make your
    answer easy—brother, as if

        you're at home—no knock at the door
        could disturb you, for who

belongs more in his place than you—a night
    like wind—into

        the rain—without
you, could this comfort remember—

    brother, when it turns actual
        is what you mean less possible—

    the rain is it itself,
or how exact it falls like grammar—kid,

    you never learn
        patterns partly—

when you can say it you tell me—
    a limit always remembers—

        the next thing you know it's hard to
        be after what you were

here for—let's have it—you leave them, brother—
    it's just the wind

        leaving the hall,
you can shut the windows later—

FIVE

PEDESTRIAN

I am a walker. I follow the sun as it angles
Into the evening on an edge where

A thoroughfare meets a hill of empty houses,
And as it spreads through back roads, I walk

Into nights—imaginary city—into nights
I walk changed, to be changed like a character

In a story I might read at the diner
On a damp morning when I don't feel right, or

By the fire, folded into fire, days or nights
Or days again, walking with a map in

My head, a little blood in my teeth. If I walk
Out into my own block and don't know

Where I am, things may even out in
Neighborhoods I've never been to as I

Begin to feel at home and forget what I am
After. I walk along the edge of the airfield.

The city swells in and out of my descriptions.
I can't make fit these words falling from

My mouth. Ships in the yard at a distance,
Then close. Clouds precede me as I walk

Home—it's not far now—between two
Memories, sidewalk shifting among

Mailboxes, streetlights, apartment complexes,
All of it settling into the orange domes

Of the synagogue, where Farmington Avenue
Dips down into the city, meets the rise of

Its buildings. This is where I'm from.
My city made real. I am elegant. Tiresome.

The avenue, I can't be precise now about how
It was then, though I see I'm still this person

In here, nestled among words. They aren't mine.
Stopping under a tree by a wall. Darkness

Cast like a light. I'm lying alone on a bench,
Feet on the arm, fingers on the sidewalk,

Buzzing with caffeine. The police come, but
I sit up and they stay in their cars. I am so

Able to be large and harmless. Thought beating
In the heart. Every yard a very varnished green.

I come and go and come and go all night. Past
The familiar gas station, through the white

Squares of the divinity school, mansion rows,
Wide and wealthy. Perhaps I depend too much

On a breeze rising unexpectedly out of
The night's heat? No matter. Long after curfew,

And I could care less which city or street.
There are rules to these things, but I've walked

Beyond them. I'm the figure in the distance.
Not everything has to be a struggle, I say.

FINAL TEA WITH HOON

Talking to myself, that's how it felt,
That's how I would say it felt
If I kept control of what I said, if I
Wasn't always amassing, out of

Control as a crowd gathering in a way
Particular to the grunge era,
Rapid and unresisting as we two
Spoke at a table, over tea, they took

Over the cool stone plaza, as if
To music, as if peanuts in
A pile, as if pickles never opened
Since 1983, as if ointment sprinkled

Golden on our beards, as if we let
The conversation be the subject, rather
If we could be subject to
The conversation, then we would not

Pass from our old lines, truck stops
And dumptrucks, with the crowd
Clasping hand to ear, and whispering
"You should've been in my shoes

Yesterday" as they began to ask
Each other's name or recognize they did
Not know how they'd found
Themselves here in the fullest part of

The morning, cool and warm and damp
With what we could still call dew.
The loneliest air hung over us.
The breeze blew through our ears.

More truly that I sat with Shannon,
And more strange that he sat
With me, all over a bowl of bitter
Beans, with everyone gone, where

We could tell what was wrong. Is
It the way we were speaking?
Is it our friends who lied?
Who died? Were you that friend

First for me, Shannon? Lost,
After having circled my arms
At the middle school dance.
Kept me calm and alone in

A hammock breeze, together
We sang gallantly.
My ears made hymns.
I was a mouthful of cavities.

And I can't stop. I feel
More myself than I ought to be.
A tide sweeps me. Like a song
In my head, I go away.

MY ROTATION

Passing faces I recognize on people I don't
Swiftly the walkway so motorized

In my anxious hour when the thought
I'm not a bunch of selves nor even one person

Who hears himself in the colonnades
Of a stadium as if an echo-y friend group

Ghosts me tells me I won't go
Alone into the cushions of the night

To wake up somebody with
Somebody else's priorities a new route to

Work which differs subtly from
The pattern of turns I've accrued

Tell me you know me see how I drive
The road fills with colors the road pools

Between curbs on the corner
Where I get in too many objects in my hands again

The road conjures a suspension thudded
Stop where a phone slides out smacks against

The edge of a cup face down between pedals
You see me how I'm one person

With many interests unpursued collecting
I suppose I don't have the time

Caught in an open lane beside and behind
Split halves of a prefabricated house

Isn't there another better option available to
Whoever this house is headed to

Some set of choices which doesn't result
In their living room bouncing

Almost out of its lane I do
The things I'm afraid to do but keep having to

Each new thing I fear becomes something
I keep fearing so that I get nowhere by

Stepping on the gas too hard pushing
My little car past a wide load just to get to

My room to my office to the seat
I'll choose at the airport bar where I feel

Weight my body pulls into itself
Down to my belt my mold one of talking

Too much waking up ambitious
Waiting for my ambitions to be filled I am

One self in rotation a face turning away from
The camera panning a field of dry grass

An abandoned picnic table a car parked in
The back of a driveway oh click if you can on

The empty moment before my face surfaces
Before I find I've started the whole thing again

AT THE COW PALACE

The balloons out of the rafters fell into
Their mass like jellyfish over
The convention center where I
Arranged the balloons in the rafters
Before they fell in my mind I felt
Those balloons settling into

Their heights rather unlike people
In our shitty bodies sloping
The open backs of folding chairs
With people the pavilions filling
So many it got dirty like
The nineties the eighties people

Pissing on a cement wall a baseball
Stadium in my head all this
If I closed my eyes turned color
Day came up on me weeks flashed
Overhead like hours passing in
A movie about bigness

I climbed from a pile of leaves
The moon tacked map blue over
The soccer field I lifted a stream
From a hose across the grass and
I held there pushed up its falling
Into soil already wet and full

POEM FOR SUSAN LEWIS

I don't know where Spencer is.
I mean I don't know where I am.
I have a picture of a church,
three sections of light. Or a rope
line. Two little dogs on it, but one at
a time. I'm in South Carolina,
with purple flowers under my sill.
Or I'm on Kenyon Street, eating

pretzels in your pantry, thank you
for the seltzer, thank you for
pulling into the breakdown lane,
thank you for everything. We're
all going to the store and I keep
walking into Spencer and he
doesn't like it. He's crying about
it and it's my fault. You talk

to him, but you don't say
a thing about me. Three sections
of light. One's bigger
than the others. None of this fits
together, and I have a better way
to make it fit, but
I'm not going to do that.
Let's say I'm a teacher. Like you.

Like Spencer. Let's put the three
of us in a room. We'll tell
these people how we don't know
how to live, but do
anyway. Let's put me on the base
of the bathtub, a pile of wrenches,
and the hot water filling up. Let's
put Spencer in the garage, with

a bag of cigarettes. Or spray paint.
Let's walk the dog, and let's watch
our step. I have a picture
of a church, three sections of light.
You be the big one. Spencer and I
can be the other two. We'll stay.
We'll have this be worth something,
even though it doesn't have to be.

IN THE CONGAREE

I'm home. I'm not home. I'm on the road or
Off it, briefly. I've been out of place. I've been

Taking familiar walks. I like the boardwalk. I like
The swamp. I feel ill at ease. I feel fine.

As August ends, I'm thick and cold. As I circle
Above a tide of cypress knees, of webs,

Fallen trunks and leaves, I gather out
The mud a mossy repose. A violent mist.

A green allure. I have spoken into
A dead and standing pool of air, where,

In its center, a spider hangs. I can hear myself
Moving, notes taken on paper, on

My feet, I stop and that makes a sound.
I look out into what feels ancient. It

Doesn't seem old. My voice is spun.
I'm rolling out myself last rung by rung.

I pinned my eye to the base of a loblolly pine,
And rose, much higher than I would

Suppose. I know everything already. I have to
Ask people questions. All of my relatives

Are famous. There are so many people dead.
Look at these trees. They're shattered in pieces.

They're tall and full. I look forward, steadily,
At the moss grown high as the flood.

TWENTIETH-FIRST CENTURY

I vote with my feet. I vote with my wallet.
I vote in person with my vote.
I have a call in to my senator's office, where

I'm almost in tears saying these words to
whoever answers the phone—it's the words
themselves, not what they call for, or where

they're from. I have a voice I can sometimes find
when my head's in a book, distracted and aware,
a voice that runs lines across a teleprompter,

clearing faces, lighting red up into gold as it
booms and twirls and fails to leave a place
for those voices inside me grown fingery

and inarticulate, too faint this time through
the copier to stand next to something so clean
and bright and blue. Blow some air out of

my lips, steal me into the kitchen—it's all metallic
and you know, I sit there. I don't put my head
in my hands. I hold it right up. All this

traveling, shifting between positions, negotiating
the anticipated movements of a crowd, or
pausing too long in the spot on

the carpet which causes the automatic doors
to open, while large shadows move across
the big-box parking lot, the cola sloshes

in a glass on deck in a storm, and the signs in
the community garden ask joggers to
keep out, as if limits weren't absurd now that

the seasons scatter their days like
pieces across some horrible game board.
I try to rest. I'm no good at it. I sit a chair down

in the shower, and put myself in with
all my clothes on. I press stacks of biographies
between my hands, walk them from

room to room. I can participate in a process,
contribute to, delighted to, I'm happy to
hand you my role. I have an aesthetic. I apply

duct-tape to my car, duct-tape to the camera, to
the listening device, to an individual notebook,
to a big stack of them—I am a person

with a thing about doing my work. The caucuses
start, and we can all see this difference
as making things the same. I'm no different.

I mean I find I have no new friends. I walk
around alone, and I can't quite tell
when I'm asleep anymore. My body carries me

to the windows of the mattress shop, lays me
against the tinted glass. I'm trying to be
a person who asks difficult questions, who one

can't get things by, but as I prepare my responses,
I find myself offering to get a cup of coffee
for a person I dislike, then a person I like, then

myself again. I leave the lines I stand in all the time.
I have no sense of these words, what
they meant to me. My eyes soften at what feels

a tender moment, but then I find I read it wrong,
it's formal, professional, an exchange
of gray-blue tones. I'm holding my hands

in the air above the keypad of an ATM machine,
unsure of my next move. I've made a political
donation or two, but it feels now like I've come out

of a fever, a hole under the blanket, the edge
of which kept coming off my toes. The bus turns
around in the lot, stops, and opens the door. The driver

says we can get off and then back on if we want.
If it were my car, I'd have a pile of glass carafes in
the back seat, aprons, work shoes, golden photos

of dewy gardens in southern New England,
elephant-colored etchings of trash heaps, a corbeil of
diplomas, some fake and some real, matted together

on the seat from the rains, because I have
no windows, no doors, no car, and nowhere
I mean to go. These are the words I walk

around with, because the ones I want
are gone. We already found them, if you remember.
We brought them out in front of everybody,
and we burned them right up.

ACKNOWLEDGMENTS

Thanks to the editors of the publications where versions of these poems first appeared: *Bennington Review, Copper Nickel, Crazyhorse, Guernica, Iowa Review, The Kenyon Review, The Literary Review, Nonsite, Phantom, Poets.org, Public Pool,* and *Salt Hill.* In addition, thanks to the editors of the anthology *Found Anew,* for which "Poem For Susan Lewis" was written. An earlier version of "Spy Poem" was published as a chapbook by Projective Industries, and an even earlier version was published as a tinyside by Big Game Books.

Thanks to Spencer Lewis, whose paintings and conversation served as the basis for several poems, especially "Red Carrying Moon." Thanks to my friends. Thanks to my teachers. Thanks to Lisa Lubasch and Max Winter. Thanks to my colleagues at the University of South Carolina. Thanks to my graduate students. Thanks to my undergraduate students. Thanks to my family. Thanks, most especially, to Liz Countryman.

ABOUT THE AUTHOR

Samuel Amadon is the author of *Like a Sea* and *The Hartford Book.* His poems have appeared in *The New Yorker, The Nation, APR, Poetry,* and *Lana Turner.* He is the director of the MFA Program in Creative Writing at the University of South Carolina, where he edits the journal *Oversound* with Liz Countryman.